THE LITTLE BOOK OF
Dialogue for Difficult Subjects

Published titles include:

The Little Book of Restorative Justice, by Howard Zehr

The Little Book of Conflict Transformation, by John Paul Lederach

The Little Book of Family Group Conferences, New-Zealand Style,
by Allan MacRae and Howard Zehr

The Little Book of Strategic Peacebuilding, by Lisa Schirch

The Little Book of Strategic Negotiation,
by Jayne Seminare Docherty

The Little Book of Circle Processes, by Kay Pranis

The Little Book of Contemplative Photography, by Howard Zehr

The Little Book of Restorative Discipline for Schools,
by Lorraine Stutzman Amstutz and Judy H. Mullet

The Little Book of Trauma Healing, by Carolyn Yoder

The Little Book of Biblical Justice, by Chris Marshall

The Little Book of Restorative Justice for People in Prison,
by Barb Toews

El Pequeño Libro De Justicia Restaurativa, by Howard Zehr

The Little Book of Cool Tools for Hot Topics,
by Ron Kraybill and Evelyn Wright

The Little Book of Dialogue for Difficult Subjects,
by Lisa Schirch and David Campt

The Little Book of Victim Offender Conferencing,
by Lorraine Stutzman Amstutz

The Little Book of Healthy Organizations,
by David R. Brubaker and Ruth Hoover Zimmerman

The Little Books of Justice & Peacebuilding
present, in highly accessible form, key concepts and
practices from the fields of restorative justice, conflict transformation, and peacebuilding. Written by leaders in these
fields, they are designed for practitioners, students, and
anyone interested in justice, peace, and conflict resolution.

The Little Books of Justice & Peacebuilding
series is a cooperative effort between the Center for Justice
and Peacebuilding of Eastern Mennonite University (Howard
Zehr, Series General Editor) and publisher Good Books
(Phyllis Pellman Good, Senior Editor).

THE LITTLE BOOK OF

Dialogue for Difficult Subjects

A Practical, Hands-On Guide

Lisa Schirch
and David Campt

Good Books

New York, New York

Cover photograph by Howard Zehr

Cover design by Dawn J. Ranck

Interior design by Cliff Snyder

THE LITTLE BOOK OF DIALOGUE FOR DIFFICULT SUBJECTS
Copyright ©2007 by Good Books, Intercourse, PA 17534
International Standard Book Number: 978-1-56148-551-2
Library of Congress Catalog Card Number: 2007038694

Good Books books may be purchased in bulk at special discounts for sales promotion, corporate gifts, fund-raising, or educational purposes. Special editions can also be created to specifications. For details, contact the Special Sales Department, Good Books, 307 West 36th Street, 11th Floor, New York, NY 10018 or info@skyhorsepublishing.com
Printed in Canada
Good Books is an imprint of Skyhorse Publishing, Inc., a Delaware corporation.®

Library of Congress Cataloging-in-Publication Data

Schirch, Lisa.
    The little book of dialogue for difficult subjects : a practical, hands-on guide / by Lisa Schirch and David Campt.
        p. cm.
    Includes bibliographical references.
    ISBN 978-1-56148-551-2 (pbk. : alk. paper) 1. Interpersonal communication.
2. Interpersonal relations. 3. Interpersonal conflict. I. Campt, David W. II. Title.
    HM1166.S34 2007
    303.6'9--dc22   2007038694

Table of Contents

Acknowledgments 3

1. Defining Dialogue 5

2. How Does Dialogue Work? 13

3. When Is Dialogue Useful? 23

4. Organizing a Dialogue Process 30

5. Designing a Dialogue Process 36

6. Facilitating a Dialogue 58

7. Moving from Dialogue to Action 65

8. Assessing Dialogue Effectiveness 71

9. Dialogue for a New Century 76

Appendix: Tools for Enlarging the Conversation 79

Endnotes 83

Recommended Reading 86

About the Authors 89

Acknowledgments

We offer a joint thank you to Hope in the Cities (HIC) in Richmond, Virginia, who hired us to co-facilitate their series of dialogues on race, economics, and jurisdiction issues. The values and vision of HIC inspire us both and we are grateful for the opportunity to work with them.

Lisa: I would like to thank my students and colleagues at the Center for Justice & Peacebuilding at Eastern Mennonite University (EMU). Over the last 10 years, as I have facilitated countless meetings on a variety of issues at EMU, my colleagues have offered helpful feedback to strengthen my facilitator skills. I have also learned a great deal by observing them facilitate dialogues on difficult subjects in which I was a participant. Along the way I've learned from them how to honestly own what I know and what I don't know, what I am skilled at, and where I can improve. I'm grateful for those colleagues who have nurtured this self-knowledge.

David: I would like to thank a collection of people, beginning with my numerous colleagues at America-Speaks, an organization that has given me the opportunity to develop my leadership skills. I'm convinced that I couldn't have co-written this book without the stimulating feedback and encouraging fellowship of Cricket White, Manny Brandt, and Theo Brown. They have inspired me to do more and learn more in the areas of dialogue. I also offer special gratitude to Moniqie Fortenberry and Ngozi Robinson, who in their unique ways have helped me maintain my sanity while making progress. And finally, nothing in my life—especially my passion for dialogue—would have happened without my parents, James and Geraldine Campt.

1.
Defining Dialogue

Most of us, if not all, can recall an uncomfortable moment at a holiday gathering when the conversation turned divisively to religion, politics, or current events. Or we have sat in a meeting or in a Sunday school class and felt tensions rising among participants. Is it just impossible for people to talk comfortably about some subjects?

Dialogue is a process for talking about tension-filled topics. It is useful for families, small groups, businesses, communities, organizations, and national and international conflicts.

Increasingly, people are seeing the need for better ways of talking. After the tragic events of September 11, 2001, community groups in various regions of the United States met to discuss that day's impact on their lives and how they might work together to prevent retaliatory violence against Muslims in their community. Other communities are using dialogue to identify guiding values for city planning and development in rapidly growing regions. In still other places, people are using dialogue to help talk about religious differences on homosexuality, community problems like youth obesity, or racial divisions among community members. In war zones, diplomats are using dialogue to explore political solutions to end civil violence.

These examples illustrate how people use dialogue to heal deep divisions or wounds from the past, avert impending violence, discuss an upcoming policy decision, or address a community challenge. People are turning to dialogue because other forms of communication fail to provide the structure or safety required for discussing difficult subjects. Dialogue helps people communicate with each other as they constructively search for creative solutions to community challenges. Dialogue is an important part of solving difficult problems and transforming relationships between adversaries.

Dialogue: A Different Kind of Communication

Definitions of dialogue abound. In popular usage, dialogue can include almost any type of verbal exchange. In Latin, dialogue refers to a conversation between two or more people, usually across lines of conflict or potential conflict. In this book, the term takes on a more specific definition.

> **Dialogue aims to build relationships between people as they address a common concern.**

Dialogue is a communication process that aims to build relationships between people as they share experiences, ideas, and information about a common concern. It also aims to help groups take in more information and perspectives than they previously had as they attempt to forge a new and broader understanding of a situation.

One way to define dialogue is to contrast it with other important and commonly used communication styles. Dialogue is different from *conversation, discussion, training or education,* and *debate.*

In *conversation,* information and ideas flow between people for the primary purpose of self-expression. Persuasion, or changing another's perspective or understanding, may not figure into the exchange. Unlike conversation, a specific goal of dialogue is to broaden participants' understanding of a particular issue.

In a *discussion,* information and ideas are exchanged in order to accomplish a specific task or to solve a problem. The intention of dialogue is not to accomplish a task, even though a dialogue process sometimes identifies follow-up tasks.

Training helps people learn something, usually by transferring knowledge from the trainer to the student. Learning also happens in dialogue, but not through a direct transfer. Dialogue helps people generate their own new collective understanding of a situation through exchanges between participants.

Debate is like a contest in which there are winners and losers. The term "debate" conjures up many images: academics battling to intellectually outdo each other's arguments, political candidates competing for votes, or heated exchanges between people at a dinner table. A culture of debate is pervasive in many places around the world.[1] In debate, participants listen to others to find what is wrong, incomplete, or otherwise flawed in their opponent's statements. The intention is to identify those flaws, expose them, and poke holes in the opponent's overall position. Many consider dialogue to be the opposite of debate.

Dialogue is a unique communication process because it focuses participants' attention on listening for understanding. Dialogue works best when participants listen for what might be correct, true, and insightful about what others have stated. The listeners try to find ideas with which they can agree, and potentially combine those with their own ideas to build a larger truth than any side has on its own. The table on page 9 highlights some of the most essential differences between dialogue and debate.

Dialogue, in its purest sense, is different from other forms of communication. Yet other communication styles can have aspects of dialogue as well. Communication is fluid and often moves in and out of various modes. A good dialogue can have the loose nature of a conversation; the focused approach to learning of a training; or the heated passion, vigor, and even anger of a debate.

While this book focuses on using dialogue with planning and intention, it is important to note that the essence of dialogue—respectful listening, learning, and sharing of experiences that shape our beliefs—can be adapted to almost any conversation involving two or more people. Accordingly, anyone can employ facilitation skills to steer a holiday dinner, meeting, or conversation away from antagonism and toward dialogue.

Dialogue: What Makes It Unique?

A Guided Process

Effective dialogue between people of diverse experiences and beliefs usually requires the guidance of a facilitator. The role of the facilitator in guiding the conversation makes dialogue different from other communication forms. Facilitators help create a safe space by setting ground rules or guidelines to keep dialogue participants focused on listening to and working with each other. Facilitators guide the dialogue process without

DEBATE	DIALOGUE
The goal is to "win" the argument by affirming one's own views and discrediting other views.	The goal is to understand different perspectives and learn about other views.
People listen to others to find flaws in their arguments.	People listen to others to understand how their experiences shape their beliefs.
People critique the experiences of others as distorted and invalid.	People accept the experiences of others as real and valid.
People appear to be determined not to change their own views on the issue.	People appear to be somewhat open to expanding their understanding of the issue.
People speak based on assumptions made about others' positions and motivations.	People speak primarily from their own understanding and experience.
People oppose each other and attempt to prove each other wrong.	People work together toward common understanding.
Strong emotions like anger are often used to intimidate the other side.	Strong emotions like anger and sadness are appropriate when they convey the intensity of an experience or belief.

deciding who is right or wrong, or declaring a "winner" as a moderator does in a debate. Chapter 6 describes the important dimensions of facilitating dialogue.

An Intention to Learn and Change
The intention behind a dialogue is its most definitive characteristic. Dialogue works best when the people involved are open to learning and changing. The role of the dialogue facilitator is to encourage this kind of attitude.

Dialogue requires a willingness to learn from those who believe differently.

Most people either consciously or unconsciously believe that there is only one right way to believe or act. For this reason, some people discredit dialogue because it requires them to recognize that they may be able to learn from people who believe differently. When people believe that they alone hold the whole truth, there is no need to listen to others.

Dialogue works best when participants bring curiosity and a sense of wonder about others, and a desire to learn more about people and their experiences. It requires humility to recognize that one person or group does not have the whole truth. In dialogue, people acknowledge that they can benefit from listening to and learning, talking, and working with others. Participants come to understand that what they believe about an issue is shaped, in part, by their life experiences and other factors such as age, class, religion, ethnicity, geography, or gender.

Openness to learning from and about others helps to create a space where people can be honest about their similarities and differences. In a dialogue process, participants are asked to respectfully listen, learn, and share their experiences with others.

A Dialogue Story

We began facilitating dialogues together in 1999 with Hope in the Cities, a nonprofit organization based in Richmond, Virginia, that works at creating just and inclusive communities.[2] As a city whose history is steeped in institutionalized slavery, Richmond was an ideal place to use dialogue to work on long-standing social divisions. We functioned as a biracial facilitator team—David, an African-American male, and Lisa, a white female—in an attempt to model cross-racial cooperation.

In 2001 we designed and guided the process for a series of weekend retreat dialogues for groups of 20 black, white, Latino, and Asian Richmonders. On one weekend a month for several years, various racially mixed groups had come together at a retreat center to share meals and lodging, relax in recreational rooms and gardens, enjoy magnificent scenery, and engage in formal and informal dialogue. During the Civil War, the mansion on the grounds had served as a hospital run by nuns that treated both Confederate and Union troops. It seemed a particularly appropriate place for honest dialogue about the city's racial, economic, and political divisions.

Those weekend dialogues used a unique format that differed from much of the work on racial reconciliation going on in the nation at the time, which involved only two- or three-hour sessions. The weekend retreat dialogue model allowed for a more intensive kind of relationship-building that fostered a greater degree of transformation. Informal rituals of eating, drinking, walking, and relaxing together—with times of ecumenical prayer as a supplement—helped to transform participants' awareness of issues of race, class, and politics in a safe and nurturing environment that was built on relationships. Ultimately, these relationships between people of different economic and racial groups are what motivate people to bring about change in their communities.

A retreat approach is just one model for facilitating dialogue. There are many others. In the following chapters, we explore how dialogue works; how to organize, design, and facilitate a dialogue process; and how to move from talk to action. We have woven short examples from our work into the chapters to demonstrate the diverse uses of dialogue.

This book identifies ways you can begin to use the process of dialogue in your family, workplace, community, and nation. With a few simple facilitation techniques, anyone can help a tense debate or conversation take on some qualities of a dialogue. Prompting people to talk about the life experiences that helped shaped their beliefs and opinions, rather than asking about the beliefs and opinions themselves, can help shift a conversation. Anyone can point out where there is common ground or similarities in opposing views. And anyone can encourage people to listen respectfully to others.

This *Little Book*, then, is useful for anyone who participates in conversation, not only for dialogue facilitators. In an age of globalization, with diverse people and societies growing increasingly interdependent, effective communication is critical. In our view, better communication leads to better understanding, which gives us the best chance of respectfully working and living together.

2.
How Does Dialogue Work?

Dialogue offers individuals and communities a variety of benefits. One way to describe how dialogue works is to say that it affects three distinct but interrelated parts of our humanity: our *intellect, emotions,* and *spirit*. Dialogue is most effective when the process addresses each of those dimensions.

Intellect

Dialogue exposes people to different ways of seeing the world. People have an opportunity to rethink their understanding and knowledge of an issue, event, or a group of people. Dialogue creates a safe space to listen and ask questions of people who have different experiences and worldviews. Recognizing the potential validity of alternative viewpoints expands people's understanding beyond their own view. For example, when environmentalists and cattle ranchers take part in a dialogue about land usage, they discover new information about each side's interests and needs.

Emotions

Dialogue prompts greater emotional understanding of others and one's own self, stirs passions, and motivates people to act. Sometimes dialogue helps people

---

identify resentments they have unknowingly carried toward individuals or groups. When it works well, dialogue helps expand people's sense of empathy for others and prompts them to act to change a situation.

For example, an intentional dialogue process between a married couple can help them learn about the historical context that shaped each spouse's emotional needs. One spouse may have developed a need for emotional space and reflection following an argument. The other may prefer to work things out as soon as possible. Dialogue can help each spouse understand the background to these different emotional needs, and can motivate the couple to try new ways of interaction given this understanding of each other's needs.

Spirit

Dialogue facilitators foster, at a minimum, a basic level of human caring for all of its participants. Though this sense of caring is not unique to dialogue settings, it is not necessarily the norm in society, especially among strangers. This experience of deep caring can expand people's sense of community connectedness.

People who are religious often characterize this sense of commonality in dialogue by saying that God is present. In a poignant description of how dialogue can touch the deeper levels of our humanity, one dialogue participant described the job of a facilitator as "doing surgery on people's souls."

How Dialogue Affects Us Individually

Dialogue often affects people in significant and lasting ways. Years after an intense dialogue between people who have felt great trauma or conflict, participants sometimes talk about how much the experience changed them. In some cases, people are touched so deeply that they change their careers to address the issues discussed in the dialogue. Many participants experience the following effects.

Personal Reflection and Clarity

A primary goal of dialogue is to help participants gain greater insight into their own perspectives, values, patterns of thinking, and biases. Most people do not realize how much their unique life experiences shape the way they believe and act. People develop different perceptions of what is "true" or "right" or "good" through their life experiences. Different perceptions or "worldviews"— ways of seeing the world—can cause disharmony and lead to interpersonal or intergroup conflicts. If a dialogue is successful, people leave the process more keenly aware of the way their personal experiences shape their perceptions, and the way their perceptions shape how they view or interpret their experiences.

One mother in a parent/teen dialogue initially complained that her daughter "whined too much" about needing praise from her. Through the dialogue and her own reflection, the mother realized that she saw her daughter as excessively wanting praise because of the way her own mother raised her. She had been taught that giving compliments lessens parental power. This is one example of how dialogue can help participants recognize their roles in the challenges they face. This space for self-reflection can lead to other changes.

Dialogue helps participants gain insight into their own perspectives.

Empathy for Others

People often prefer to be with others they perceive as similar to themselves. People who see themselves as significantly different from another person or group create boundaries that distinguish "us" from "them." The less people interact with each other, the more they are likely to perceive each other as strange, wrong, or even evil. A fundamental goal of dialogue is to explore participants' experiences and perceptions so they can potentially understand why those in different groups may view reality differently.

In the ethnically divided Fijian islands, indigenous leaders are often in conflict with Indo-Fijian (originally from India) business and community leaders. These tensions have erupted into political coups on several occasions. In an interethnic national peace dialogue in Fiji, participants shared with each other their most important needs and interests in finding a peaceful solution to these tensions. In the process, people learned to empathize with the experiences of others and discovered similarities they didn't know existed previous to the dialogue. Dialogue provided the context for indigenous and Indo-Fijians to share their experiences living through several violent political coups. People in both groups told stories of anxiety and tension caused by the political turmoil. The dialogue created a sense of shared history and community in times of hardship.[3]

Increased Understanding

In dialogue, understanding why people believe what they believe, in the context of their stories, is central. Some may regard reports or facts generated by journalists or researchers as more objective measures of truth than personal stories. But dialogue helps participants to understand that both types of knowledge are valuable, and that neither are totally objective.

Participants in the interracial dialogues in Richmond reflected on their own lives, especially on ways they experienced economic, racial, and jurisdictional segregation in the region. As time progressed, we saw significant shifts among participants in how they understood the impact of race on economic and political divisions in their city. In general, African Americans tended to be more acutely aware of this impact because of their own experiences. Nevertheless, the dialogue prompted

Dialogue values both "objective facts" and personal stories in understanding an issue.

some white citizens to realize that they and some blacks shared a semi-conscious frustration about the way some parts of town were considered "off-limits" for whites on weekend nights.

How Dialogue Affects Groups and Communities

Many people who engage in dialogue do so because of the positive effects it can have on groups of people and entire communities. The strength of these changes varies widely, but includes the following five interrelated effects.

Reduced Divisions

Conflict is a fundamental part of the human condition. By its nature, conflict produces at least a temporary sense of division between people who see a situation differently and who view each other as obstacles to their own goals.

In some situations, conflict produces a real division between people. They see others as different than or less than themselves. These deep divisions make it difficult to achieve a sense of common purpose, and make future conflicts more likely to be handled in destructive ways.

Dialogue is used not only to solve an immediate and pressing conflict but also to directly address these deeper, historical divisions between individuals and groups. Dialogue offers opportunities to bring people together to reflect on their shared humanity and common ground.

Many churches use dialogue as a process for addressing internal divisions. People within the same congregation may have different views on homosexuality, styles of worship, abortion, or divorce. Sometimes the divisions become so deep that the congregation divides into two or more new churches. Dialogue can help a congregation discern both the different sets of experiences and expressions of faith that divide them, as well as assess the unity or common ground that exists.

In a parent/teen dialogue among black participants, some adults remarked that they had never fully realized the stresses their teenagers faced, including skepticism they felt from white students about their academic abilities, and pressures from their black peers not to exert maximum effort academically. Most importantly, the adults realized that they may not have done a very effective job of openly listening to their own teenager, inadvertently causing additional stress. Dialogue helped these parents better understand student stresses, thereby reducing the divisions between parents and their children.[4]

A Sense of Community

In North-American society, people increasingly lead independent lives, rarely knowing or relating to their neighbors. Dialogue can build relationships where people have no established patterns of relating to each other. Dialogue can help create a sense of cohesion among disparate people, largely because dialogue begins with people sharing their experiences.

A palpable sense of togetherness or unity develops when people find similarities between their own experiences and the stories of others. Dialogue does more than gather together very different people; it intentionally works at building a sense of community.

> **Dialogue builds a sense of togetherness among disparate people.**

After the tragic events of September 11, 2001, people around the United States gathered to talk about the events with their neighbors. The tragedy brought people together in new ways. Strangers reached out to talk to each other, to listen to the suffering of others, and to find ways to help. After 9/11, some communities planned formal dialogues to more intentionally find ways to express trauma and create paths toward community healing and unity.

Improved Communication Patterns

Dialogue facilitators model and encourage participants to develop a wide range of skills that include: active listening, speaking honestly and assertively about experiences and opinions while remaining sensitive to others, following group ground rules for communicating effectively, and identifying common ground. The attitudes and skills needed in dialogue are useful for improving communication in many settings, and are the foundation of all conflict transformation and peacebuilding processes.

Several participants involved in the parent/teen dialogues reported that tensions within their households had palpably eased. Parents responded that they had become much more patient listeners, and teens reported that they were less quick to "give attitude" to their parents. In addition, many parents reported that they previously had little support from other parents, and that they were committed to staying connected with other parents after the dialogue ended.

Dialogue can affect communication patterns on both individual and group levels. Many institutions have used dialogue trainings and experiences to change the way they deal with conflict and make decisions with stakeholders. For example, a health maintenance organization (HMO) with 100,000 clients underwent an organizational training in dialogue skills that was intended not only to improve the capacity of its medical staff to work more cooperatively, but also to communicate with patients more effectively.[5]

Collective Analysis

Community leaders and policymakers have few tools for assessing what the public thinks about a problem. Opinion polls show whether respondents agree or disagree with education policies, but polls cannot provide leaders with real insight into what parents think are the root problems in education or elicit creative ideas for solving them.

Dialogue is a way for people to collaboratively identify the most important issues affecting a group. It may help a group to understand how and why some people feel excluded from community decision-making. In other cases, dialogue may help people get more in touch with their dissatisfaction with a situation so that they are motivated to get involved in activities focused on change.

When using dialogue on issues involving large numbers of people, dozens or even hundreds of small-group dialogues are arranged—sometimes at one place. Electronic technologies allow hundreds of people to engage in small-group processes, and for each small group to electronically share its important analytical observations and creative ideas for collective action.[6]

In 2002, 4,300 people gathered in New York City for a dialogue about the redevelopment of the World Trade Center site. Coordinators of the event had tried to ensure sufficient representation by survivors of the 9/11 attack, relatives of those who had died, neighborhood storeowners, and local residents. In a turn of events that surprised almost everyone, the people gathering expressed distaste for of all the six redevelopment plans that had been proposed. After the meeting, the local development authority commissioned a new set of plans that were intended to more faithfully follow the preferences expressed within the dialogue.[7]

Options for Collaborative Action

Collective analysis paves the way for collective action. The dialogue process itself often provides an inspirational model for how a community can harness its diversity for constructive change. As people experience a small version of their ideal dream community in the dialogue process, they get excited and energized to help create better relationships and communication patterns outside the dialogue process.

For example, dialogues on development, urban sprawl, and community growth bring diverse people from the community together—farmers, immigrants, business leaders, parents, and many others—to find solutions. The inherent diversity of stakeholders' experiences is essential for undertaking a thoughtful analysis of current and potential problems of community development decisions. The collective needs and desires of all members of a community provide the best guides for making smart growth and development decisions, such as where to build schools, housing, and shopping centers.

The collective wisdom of all members helps guide the best decisions.

Dialogue prepares a group to take collective action—or at least to have a healthy exploration of whether such action is possible. Dialogue provides space for people to express their experiences, perspectives, and preferences for action and gives leaders a more reliable sense of what key stakeholders want. This, in turn, reduces division, enhances a group's sense of identity, and yields emotional and spiritual benefits. In addition, the collective wisdom, analysis, and visions for the future that emerge from dialogue among diverse people open the door for other possibilities.

3.
When Is Dialogue Useful?

This chapter explores when dialogue is useful and the necessary preconditions for a successful dialogue. It details the different forms dialogue takes, from structuring a weekly Sunday-school class to using it in a conference setting.

Preconditions for a Successful Dialogue Process

The nearly infinite variations and uses of dialogue make hard-and-fast rules difficult. Yet some conditions are particularly helpful.

A Diversity of Experiences

If a primary purpose of dialogue is to help people examine their own and others' perceptions, ideas, and understandings, then it is critical that participants bring diverse experiences. A dialogue on homosexuality within a church, for example, will lead to greater understanding and growth if it includes people from different perspectives, orientations, experiences, and religious understandings.

If it is impossible to gather people who hold diverse views on an issue, the benefits of holding a dialogue around that issue likely will be diminished. Such scenarios require more skill from the facilitator, who must find ways to bring unrepresented experiences and per-spectives into the discussion. The degree of transfor-mation in a dialogue is largely related to the level of diversity in the group, as participants see that different experiences lead to different perspectives on the same issue.

No Immediate Decisions Need to be Made

Dialogues are usually more successful when no im-minent decision is required. Dialogue can help create the conditions for collaborative action, but is most ef-fective when there is no pressure for immediate action.

To a large extent, dialogue is about discovery; participants explore their perspectives around a topic, probe what might lie beneath their differ-ences and similarities, then try to discover whether there is any basis for common action.

> **Dialogue is about discovery.**

Urgency or pressure to act tends to reduce partici-pants' patience with the process of exploration and dis-covery. This impatience makes people less capable of doing the deep listening that dialogue requires.

Furthermore, when a group is pressed to make a deci-sion, the focus turns to generating and analyzing facts that are seen as relevant to the decision. In the process of decision-making, the group loses focus on the varied experiences of the participants and the implications of those differences.

While we offer this caution, we also note that dialogue is useful to deescalate tensions in situations of impend-ing conflict or violence. This was the case in Cincin-nati, Ohio, in April 2001, when tensions between law enforcement and the community boiled over after police shot an unarmed person. A large-scale effort took place to address police/community relations, using dialogue processes to talk within racial groups and across racial lines. The dialogues resulted in a set of citizen recommendations about what might be done to improve relationships between communities and the police force. In this context, dialogue helped to reduce tensions and create a safe space for people to build relationships across the lines of conflict.[8]

Relatively Balanced Power

Ideally, participants of a dialogue should have relatively equal levels of power. Dialogue is more difficult when individuals in one group are perceived as having more power from education, wealth, or social position than individuals in other groups. Significant power imbalances tend to undermine a group's capacity to dialogue. This is particularly true if the dialogue occurs as a precursor to potential joint action in which some dialogue members have more power to shape the actions the group might take.

In settings where power is uneven among participants, those with more power are likely to be taken more seriously than those with less power. Conversely, less powerful members of the group may psychologically disengage from the process and/or resent the more powerful members. They may sense that the exchanges in the dialogue are merely a false ritual to prepare everyone for what the more powerful members intend to do anyway.

Similarity in Perceived Language Capacity

Dialogues are more successful when people share similar abilities in their capacity to express their thoughts, emotions, and spirit through words. Experience, education, age, or language background may make some people perceive themselves or others as less capable of expressing themselves verbally.

In the interracial dialogues we facilitated, participants with less formal education spoke less often. In discussions with those participants, we learned that they kept quiet because they thought the participants with more formal education could talk about the issues in "a fancy way." This became a major issue, as one goal was to create partnerships across all the lines of division in the city, including race and class. While the dialogues were able to bridge race lines, we had greater challenges in crossing class and education lines.

If possible, it is important to avoid putting groups with vastly different language capacities together. For example, some dialogue specialists do not put youth and adults in the same small-group setting. To bridge language differences that reflect education levels, some dialogue specialists incorporate nonverbal communication techniques, such as drawing or group games, to help put everyone on equal footing.

Types of Dialogue

Dialogue takes a variety of forms according to diverse needs. Dialogue can be used interpersonally, as a one-time event, within a larger event like a conference, in a series of meetings, or as a sustained process over many years.

One-On-One or Small-Group Informal Dialogue
Anyone can use dialogue skills informally to ease discussions on difficult subjects. Dialogue can take place if one or more people in a discussion can use facilitation skills to model good communication, listening, and an attitude of learning from others' experiences.

One-Time Dialogue
Dialogue can be incorporated into a one-time event like a conference or retreat to *explore a special topic.* Workshops or seminars can use a dialogue format to help participants share experiences and explore a particular theme. Or a conference can include a block of time in which all participants join small groups to dialogue with the help of facilitators.

A one-time dialogue process can be used to *address a conflict* that is reaching a boiling point. Dialogue allows people on different sides of a conflict to hear each other more clearly than they might otherwise. The presence of facilitators and the use of small-group conversations often minimize public grandstanding and distorted depictions of opposing positions that often happen in public meetings designed to address tensions. In addition, dialogue is valuable in helping people witness the "other side's" interest in increasing community harmony.

One-time dialogues are also useful for *gathering information.* Bringing together hundreds or thousands of people for a one-time dialogue or "town-hall meeting" can help organizers to quickly assess stakeholders' preferences.

Another purpose of one-time dialogues is to *further mobilize a community.* If the organizers have successfully generated interest from the press, gathering together a large group of people for dialogue helps increase a community's awareness of an issue. In addition, as people experience authentic dialogue around difficult issues with people unlike themselves, they are more likely to galvanize new support for community change.

Dialogue with Multiple Sessions
Many organizations use a series of three to eight dialogues as a way to address ongoing community issues. Although most difficult community issues could benefit from more sessions, participants are not likely to sign on for an open-ended process. Thus, limiting the number of sessions makes it easier to solicit participation.

Sustained Dialogue
Some dialogue processes have no defined ending. Open-ended dialogue processes are sometimes called learning communities or support groups that intentionally use dialogue in their meetings. In many cases, open-ended dialogues grow out of a dialogue series that has excited participants about the power of such exchanges.

For example, during the 1980s, citizens of the Soviet Union and the United States held an ongoing, open-ended dialogue. For years, facilitators brought together people from the two countries in an effort to build positive relationships and deescalate tensions. Harold Saunders, a dialogue expert who facilitated many of these exchanges, called these open-ended dialogues "sustained dialogue."[9] *Sustained dialogue* is helpful in situations where the problems or conflicts are deeply rooted in history and in people's perceptions of their identity, religion, or culture; and where the conflict is complex, involving many stakeholders.

Large-Scale Dialogue

Large-scale dialogues can include hundreds or even thousands of people in centrally organized, simultaneous, small-group conversations. In contrast to a typical town meeting where only a relatively few people can speak, a coordinated large-scale dialogue gives all participants a chance to express their perspectives. Large-scale dialogues give people a more palpable sense of "community" writ large.

Using highly skilled facilitators and technologies such as teleconferencing, organizations like AmericaSpeaks lead processes for large communities or cities. A process involving 1,000 people may organize participants into 100 dialogue tables of 10 people each. In New Orleans, for example, AmericaSpeaks organized two dialogues involving 2,500 in December 2006 and 1,300 people in January 2007 to ensure that both the citizens remaining in the city and those living in other cities could examine emerging plans for city rebuilding. These meetings gave city planners and pubic officials concrete feedback about citizen perspectives on key issues. The dialogues also began to rebuild trust among the public in the planning process itself. After the second meeting, residents recommended that the city convene quarterly and hold annual dialogue-based meetings to get citizen input in the recovery process.

In large-scale dialogue, participants and organizers can have a more accurate sense of stakeholders' diverse needs. If people feel included and truly heard, they may be less likely to resist group decisions that oppose their positions.

4.
Organizing a Dialogue Process

While anyone can create informal dialogues in one's home, organization, or business, larger and more formal dialogues require a team effort. It begins with assessing individual strengths and dividing responsibilities accordingly. Specifically, the roles include *dialogue organizer, dialogue designer,* and *dialogue facilitator.*

Dialogue organizers/promoters coordinate invitations for people to attend the dialogue. The organizing role also involves managing the logistics and atmosphere of the dialogue process.

Dialogue designers develop the sequence of steps in the dialogue process. This includes developing the questions for leading the group through the topic. It also involves planning other interactions for the participants, such as introductions, a discussion of ground rules, or group meals and activities.

Dialogue facilitators guide participants through the dialogue process. Usually the facilitator works from a dialogue plan created by the designer, and carefully makes decisions about when to stray from that design.

This chapter primarily discusses the tasks of a dialogue organizer/promoter, whose role is to develop a strategy for persuading people to be part of a dialogue. Some people make good facilitators because they are calm and balanced. These same people may be less skilled in effectively promoting a dialogue or persuading someone to participate in the process, which requires generating and conveying enthusiasm. As a team defines leadership roles, it is useful to keep these distinct roles in mind. As important as it is to design a first-rate dialogue process and to involve highly skilled facilitators, these are meaningless if the efforts to organize and promote the dialogue are not successful.

Several points apply when organizing most dialogues: Develop savvy marketing plans, choose a strategic location for the dialogues, and deploy a team that wisely capitalizes on people's diverse strengths.

Marketing a Dialogue Process

Convincing people to join a dialogue process takes effort. Dialogue is a somewhat unnatural process, particularly in cultures that prefer heated debates, discussions of how to accomplish specific tasks, or trainings focused on disseminating information. Dialogue is different than all of these in that the focus is on collaborative learning.

A savvy marketing plan can persuade people to join a dialogue process.

Organizers can learn how to persuade people to join a dialogue process by borrowing marketing strategies that corporations use to sell their products. The product is the dialogue process. Businesses know that they need to appeal to consumers' needs and interests. Similarly, dialogue marketing strategies should be tailored to specific audiences. The following set of questions may help identify the best way to frame a dialogue to persuade diverse groups to join.

1. Who are the constituency groups that you want represented in the dialogue?

2. What does each constituency group identify as its current needs or interests regarding the dialogue topic?

3. Why might each constituency group be interested in joining a dialogue process? What will its members get out of it?

4. What marketing message will most likely appeal to each constituency and motivate its members to join the dialogue process?

For example, some communities are motivated to participate in dialogue because they want politicians to hear the will of the people. In other communities, the idea of people coming together across lines of conflict might hold more appeal as a marketing message. A savvy dialogue promoter tailors the messages used to publicize the event based on stakeholders' unique needs.

Because dialogue differs significantly from typical forms of communication, it is essential that invitations strike the right tone. Few adults are excited about signing up for a process that promises to change them. By contrast, people may be more receptive to the idea that they will learn how other people think on an issue, or that they will have a chance to explain to others how they think.

The Invitation Process

Using flyers, posters, or email solicitations to invite people to a dialogue are often unproductive. Many dialogue organizers find face-to-face persuasion the best way to invite people to a dialogue process. Organizers can invite key leaders first, then invite others using the commitment of participation from others as a selling point. Committed participants in a proposed dialogue may also be asked to suggest names or extend invitations to others they think should be included.

When dialogue is task-focused, broadly advertising dialogue as a necessary step in a problem-solving process may effectively recruit participants. However, a task-focused invitation creates expectations of a quick "solution," and may undermine participants' willingness to patiently explore the details of people's experiences.

Transparency about the duration of the process is important. It is better to start small and go for reenlistment than to try signing people into a lengthy process or extending it beyond the initial agreement.

Diversity

Significant care and resources must be expended to ensure all stakeholders in a community are present. In very large dialogues with multiple subgroups or dialogue tables, it is important to have a strategy that guarantees diversity in each small group. People tend to come to dialogues with people like themselves, and usually are hesitant to sit down at a table of strangers. A system of random seat assignment with gentle enforcement is important.

Choosing Dialogue Space

The space in which a dialogue is held needs to be neutral, both symbolically and logistically. The choice of venue should not inadvertently give some participants an advantage over others. Care in choosing a location can reassure people's sense of fairness and equality before the process even begins.

Sometimes dialogues may require more than one venue. For example, in a sustained dialogue between Muslims and Christians, it may be wise to alternate between meeting in a church and a mosque.

When choosing a venue, symbolic associations matter. Some locations may be currently occupied or controlled by neutral institutions, but have a historical association with one or another side of an issue. It is vital that dialogue organizers consciously examine how a location affects different potential dialogue participants.

Food, Time, and Aesthetics

Attention to hospitality, such as making food and drink available, helps people relax and gives them something to do as they interact with each other at breaks. A beautiful and comfortable space also helps people relax enough to consider multiple points of view and to see the humanity in others.[10]

Scheduling dialogue sessions requires a sensitivity to members' varying job schedules, child-care availability, transportation options, and other aspects that may affect participation. Avoid scheduling sessions in a way that consistently compromises one group's ability to attend.

Good, Trained Facilitation

Dialogue organizers also oversee the selection and training of dialogue facilitators. The quality of participants' experience is dependent on the quality of facilitation they experience. It is important to recruit facilitators who are reasonably experienced in this role and to offer them a brief training in the dialogue design so they are clear on the objectives of each small-group conversation. Given their role in the process, it is essential to make them feel sufficiently appreciated before, during, and after the event.

In large dialogues with multiple facilitators, a lead facilitator should convene, manage, guide, and conclude the experience from a main stage. In many cases, a small team of lead facilitators is used to demonstrate diversity in the leadership process. The person or people in this role must be able to effectively command the attention of dozens or hundreds of people. They should convey confidence and even passion about the process itself; be thoroughly familiar with the design so that they can make decisions about adjustments that might be needed; and convey a calm, likable presence.

Ideally, dialogue organizers choose their facilitators early in the process, so the facilitators can be involved in the dialogue design, which is the focus of the next chapter.

5.
Designing a
Dialogue Process

There are no hard-and-fast rules for designing a dialogue process. However, our experience identifies a few essential components that underlie most successful dialogue models. Successful dialogues have four general components or phases:

> Phase 1: Establishing Common Intentions and Norms
> Phase 2: Sharing Experiences and Perceptions
> Phase 3: Exploring Diversity and Commonalities
> Phase 4: Exploring Possibilities for Action

Phase 1: Establishing Common Intentions and Norms

People tend to question other people's motives when they are in conflict. This phase of dialogue establishes a group's common intention to listen and learn from each other.

Many people have never participated in an intentionally designed dialogue process. Some cultural norms for communication run counter to the kind of deep listening and honest engagement required in dialogues. For many people, practicing these skills feels as foreign as trying to write one's name with the opposite hand.

Setting norms, guidelines, or ground rules for dialogue helps prepare participants for this unique experience and signals that they may need to improvise or try out new ways of communicating. Groups whose participants already know each other may have high-quality communication in place and may not need to explicitly discuss these expectations. But groups of strangers almost always need some guidance about how they will engage with each other in this new, potentially unfamiliar communication setting.

There are three elements to establishing norms. These are *creating a safe space, setting ground rules,* and *clarifying the role of the facilitator.*

Creating Safe Space

At the outset of a dialogue, a facilitator's primary task is to help each person feel emotionally safe and offer reassurance that the facilitator will guard against verbal attacks or humiliation of participants during the dialogue. People's perceptions of a facilitator's personality and skills in creating this safe space are important. For example, the dialogue designer may call for the facilitator

Ensuring a safe place for each person puts participants at ease.

to greet participants upon arriving and connect one-on-one with them before the session starts. This can go a long way in putting people at ease.

Introducing the dialogue's goal and focus helps to create safety for participants who may feel confused, uncertain, or tense. Clearly stating the purpose helps people to understand what is expected of them and helps them to relax.

Participant introductions are also essential in creating safe space. People want to know who else is present in the dialogue, where they are from, and perhaps some organizational affiliation, such as where they work or go to church. Perhaps the most essential aspect of introductions is giving participants an opportunity to say and hear from others about why they chose to participate in the dialogue. Introductions that ask people to share their motivations for joining the dialogue can help build trust, increase empathy among participants, and establish shared positive motivation. It is one of the most useful activities in the initial phase of a dialogue because it allows participants to connect with each other on their highest motivations for being involved in the process. In addition, it gives each participant experience in expressing his/her perspective within the setting.

Some people tend to doubt others' motivations. An even stronger tendency is for people to put the best possible spin on their own motivations. They may say, for example, that they want to "learn about others." Usually people on all sides of an issue find that they share this goal.

Another useful technique for introductions is to ask participants to state something about themselves that is essentially unrelated to the topic at hand. Some examples are a hobby, a childhood nickname, number of siblings, a favorite artist or performer, or an attribute about themselves that usually surprises people. This exercise reminds people that each person is a unique human being and not just a member of a group related to a problem. Facilitators should decide how personal or whimsical to make this. For example, in a tense corporate setting, it may not be productive to ask people to reveal childhood nicknames. Whatever the question, it is important to use the same question for everyone.

Ground Rules or Guidelines

An additional technique for establishing safety and a good environment for dialogue involves setting ground rules immediately after introductions. Ground rules—sometimes also called dialogue guidelines—are a set of behavioral standards and goals that the group agrees to follow to create the best possible experience. Ground rules are important for several reasons.

First, setting ground rules serves to normalize an unusual process. In dialogue, the group designs and agrees to its own set of norms and guidelines. This is a unique aspect of dialogue. Rarely

> **Setting ground rules helps a group identify the behaviors it wants to protect.**

are social norms articulated or agreed upon by shared consensus. In sporting events, everyone expects rules of engagement, but someone else sets and enforces the rules. Setting guidelines together helps participants consciously choose to engage in the process and decide what behaviors to honor and protect.

Secondly, setting guidelines together communicates that everyone in the group is essentially equal, at least with respect to the group's task. This is also somewhat rare because most settings in which people interact involve some degree of hierarchy where someone is in authority over others. If the dialogue is based upon a collaborative search for truth among participants, it is vital that all of those involved have equal opportunity to participate fully in the process and no one is seen as the authority.

Generally, there are two ways to set ground rules. In a setting with time constraints, one approach is to list the ground rules and ask if people can comply with them. It is important that each person has a chance to modify or raise concerns about the rules. Beware of prematurely assuming that people have agreed to a set of ground rules when they have not. After ample opportunity to change the proposed ground rules, the facilitator can invite public agreement that the participants are willing to hold themselves and others accountable to the ground rules. Clearly, this is the most time-efficient

---

Sample of Basic Ground Rules

1. *Recognize the power of deep listening.* Listen to understand the other's point of view rather than to prepare a defense of your own view. Try to listen more than you speak.

2. *Respect others and refuse to engage in name-calling.* People have the right to define themselves, but not others.

3. *Speak about personal experiences.* Start your sentences with "I" rather than "you." "I experienced...."

4. *Minimize interruptions and distractions.* In general, people should be allowed to finish what they are saying without being interrupted directly or with side-talk between other participants. Also, people should silence their cell phones.

5. *Maintain confidentiality.* Outside the group, participants may discuss the content of what was said, not who said what.

---

strategy and allows the facilitator to quickly move into the dialogue.

Another approach is to elicit the ground rules from the group. When people invest thought and energy in developing ground rules, they are more likely to adhere to them. But the process can be very time consuming. Eliciting ground rules can be a helpful way to learn the concerns, fears, and other tendencies in the group.

We have separated the basic ground rules from those that might help groups go deeper.

Ground Rules for Going Deeper

1. *Ask questions.* Ask honest, thought-provoking questions that give people the opportunity to explore and explain their underlying assumptions.

2. *Stay through the hard times.* Make a commitment to stay in the dialogue despite the tensions.

3. *Aim to understand.* The goal of dialogue is to increase understanding between individuals. The goal is not to solve the problem or agree on everything.

4. *Recognize common ground.* Every two people share something in common. Find it!

5. *"Ouch," then educate.* If someone says something hurtful, don't just disengage. Let the individual and the group know why it was hurtful.

One strategy to align the group around ground rules is to ask, "Before we go any further, can we all agree to stay respectful and give everybody a chance to speak?" People will rarely say no, and this question gives you and others the capacity to point out when people are being disrespectful and are interrupting. Potentially the group agreement on this question can empower the facilitator to point out when some people are dominating the conversation.

Clarifying the Facilitator Role

A facilitator guides people through a dialogue process. Facilitators are process experts rather than experts on a subject area. They keep a dialogue focused, help participants consider a variety of views, and summarize group discussions. They model active listening and respectful speaking.

Chapter 6 details how to facilitate a dialogue. When explaining the role of a facilitator to a group, some of the more important points to clarify are these:

- Facilitators help the group explore similarities and differences of opinion. Facilitators do not promote or share their own opinions.

- Facilitators make sure that all participants get a chance to contribute to the dialogue.

- Facilitators bear primary responsibility for enforcing the ground rules, although the group also shares this responsibility collectively.

Phase 2: Sharing Experiences and Perceptions

The second key component in dialogue design is sharing experiences. People often do not recognize that every person experiences life in a unique way. Learning in dialogue comes through exploring the similarities and differences in the experiences of people from different backgrounds. In the best circumstances, people see that their beliefs about an issue are shaped by their unique experiences, and that others' different understandings or opinions often grow out of different experiences.

Warming Up

The facilitator should have a general plan for how to get past introductions and into the topic. Before the group begins to probe the difficult aspects of a topic, it is often useful to ask people to share an experience related to the topic. For example, "Describe an early time in your life when you felt like an outsider." Such a question works well early in the dialogue for a number of reasons.

First, these types of questions are educational and evoke empathy as people relate to experiences of vulnerability. Second, if the dialogue is made up of "insiders," or majorities, and "outsiders," or minorities, people in the minority may have never heard of someone in the majority feeling like an outsider. Minority or "out-group" members recognize the "in-group" status of others, and often think a person's status is fixed. Dynamics among children make "outsider" experiences almost universal. It is useful for out-group members to recognize that everyone can relate, at some level, to being an outsider.

Getting and Staying Personal

Facilitators need to pose a neutral question or a set of questions that requires participants to explore their experiences. For example, a dialogue on homosexuality might begin with a neutral question such as "How did you first learn about homosexuality?" A dialogue on community development might begin with a question such as "Share a story about a time when this community really worked well together."

Dialogue requires clear and open-ended questions that allow every participant to share an experience that is relevant to the topic. The questions should elicit an entire set of stories that highlights the diversity of the issues. It is essential that the questions help the group honor every person's experience as valuable additions.

Ideally, each participant will share in some depth about his or her *own* experiences. Facilitators may need to remind people not to stray into speculating how other people believe or to generalize their own experiences to others in their group. The goal is to get beyond stereotypes. The following types of questions can help keep people focused on telling their own stories.

Involving All Participants

The questions should not privilege any one group or focus on the experiences of only some participants. It is important that the facilitator show authentic interest in every person and ensure that all experiences are heard.

Sample Questions for Sharing Experiences

- How has this issue/conflict impacted you personally?
- How are you coping with this issue?
- What is your greatest concern about this issue now?

For example, as a first question in a dialogue about race relations, asking "What did your parents teach you about race?" is generally more helpful than asking "What did your parents teach you about racial oppression?" The question about racial oppression might encourage the group who has experienced racial oppression to share their stories, and may inhibit those who have not experienced racial oppression. The phrasing of the question itself suggests that certain people in the room have experiences that are more real and/or relevant to the topic than other participants.

Phrasing questions with a perceived bias has numerous negative consequences for the group. First, it reinforces stereotypes rather than helps people think beyond them. Group members who feel that their experiences are not valued may withdraw from participating, either by leaving the group altogether or by "checking out" psychologically. Once this happens, those who chose to share their experiences may feel that they were "put on display" by the process and become resentful themselves.

Clearly, these dynamics can become destructive to individuals and to the group. To maximize dialogue's potential, each member of the group must feel like he or she has something valuable to contribute.

Adding Analysis to Sharing Experiences
One risk during this stage is that some participants will begin to add their analysis or opinions of a problem when they share their personal experiences. Facilitators can encourage participants to stay focused on describing their own experiences while listening and asking questions of other participants' experiences. Yet the

facilitator does not want to shut down the discussions. Such comments are part of the overall education of each participant.

If this phase is handled well, participants recognize how experiences shape perceptions or opinions of the issue at hand. Some participants might resist this idea. A few will blame or doubt others whose experiences have led to different opinions than their own. Phase 3 gives participants a chance to explore why people have different experiences and perceptions.

Phase 3: Exploring Diversity and Commonalities

Once participants have had a chance to share their experiences, the dialogue then moves to helping participants identify the underlying conditions that account for their different experiences and perceptions. People tend to see their own perspectives and experiences as "the truth" and other's perspectives as "wrong." In Phase 3, participants collectively examine, "Why are our experiences and perceptions so different?"

Hopefully by this point the participants share an emotional bond with each other, and are less inclined to dismiss each other's perspectives about divisive issues. If the dialogue has gone well, the participants heard perspectives that do not fit easily into their preconceived notions, and are willing to join others in finding a larger understanding of the truth.

This phase focuses on helping people reexamine everyone's experiences in a larger context. In Phase 2, the central question was "What was your experience?" In Phase 3, the central question is "What factors cause us to have different experiences and different perspectives?"

Sample questions, such as the ones below help participants recognize differences and similarities between individuals and subgroups within a dialogue. They raise awareness about how people's perceptions shape their interpretations of reality. Participants explore influences that have shaped a problem; ideally, this helps them see their own role in a problem.

Sample Questions for Exploring the Diversity of Experiences

- How is the conflict/issue affecting our community?

- What changes are we seeing?

- How has the conflict affected how we work together? Are there new tensions among us?

- What is the wound that keeps us from addressing the issue?

- What values in our community can we draw on to address this problem?

- What are the causes of the conflict?

- What is the history of the problem?

- Do we have different understandings of the issue's history among us?

- What are the three most powerful forces fueling the issue/conflict?

Caucuses

Sometimes separating dialogue participants into subgroups or "caucuses" of people with similar experiences may be helpful in this phase. Caucuses can help participants more fully explore potentially sensitive dialogue themes. In a family dialogue, for example, a facilitator could caucus with the children and parents separately to ensure that the children are empowered to articulate their experiences and needs. In a dialogue on racial divisions, caucuses may help groups safely explore facts, ideas, and/or behaviors in a comfortable group before discussing them with the "other" group.

When discussing particularly divisive subjects, the greater level of honesty in a caucus can help move a dialogue forward. For example, a caucus used in a dialogue between members of a divided church could ask each subgroup to develop three questions they'd like to ask the other group. Caucus discussions can be summarized and brought back to the large group to accelerate progress on key issues.

Before probing these questions directly, make sure that participants acknowledge the group's diverse experiences and perspectives. In some cases, the exchanges

---

Suggested Caucus Questions

- What do we need to know from an opposing point of view in order to address this issue?

- How does our group benefit from and suffer from the status quo?

---

in Phase 2 will make this quite plain for everyone. In other cases, the facilitator needs to highlight the similarities and differences in people's experiences so everyone can see them. This process of lifting up the group's similarities and differences can help transition between Phases 2 and 3.

As people begin to sort out the diversity of narratives expressed in Phase 2, they often raise the issue of *perception*. People or groups may suggest that others are paranoid, and thus see mistreatment where there might be other explanations for people's behavior. Conversely, some will argue that other groups just don't "get it" and are blind to obvious dynamics.

The facilitator does not necessarily need to settle this issue, but rather to manage the atmosphere so that the participants can work through these perceptions and develop a shared understanding of the differences. The facilitator may acknowledge that perceptions generally play *some role* in the creation of our experiences. The primary job of the facilitator is to help construct a fair and honest exploration of the question.

An additional task of the facilitator is to help the participants step back and see that none of them has created the problem. The issue (in most cases) was not created by the people in the dialogue. Rather, it was most likely created by a combination of historical or institutional actions, and has been handed down over time and across distances and groups. The facilitator may need to remind participants of these larger factors that create different experiences and perceptions.

A final task in Phase 3 is helping participants see that even though they have inherited the problem, they may choose to perpetuate or change it. The facilitator's goal is to help participants see a connection between their own perspectives and behaviors, and the forces that perpetuate the problem. In this way, the dialogue highlights that each participant is an agent for change.

The Role of Independent Research and Statistics
In the Richmond dialogues on race, we began each weekend retreat with a factual presentation on the different educational, employment, housing, and transportation opportunities available to black, white, Latino, and Asian people in the city. These statistics, generated and presented by a local university professor, helped dialogue participants recognize various disparities between racial groups in the city. The facts provided a starting point for the dialogue.

In some cases, a presentation of facts may distract from a dialogue process. Several considerations help determine the benefits and the risks of presenting facts in a dialogue.

Benefits of an Initial Focus on Facts
Depending on the strategy used to recruit people into the process, some participants may not have much knowledge about the topic but may have chosen to attend because someone they trust invited them. Presenting facts helps raise awareness about the issues.

If facts will eventually play a major role in the group's exchanges, there can be great benefit in creating a common baseline of foundational knowledge from the outset. This makes it less likely that people will bring to the dialogue "facts" that may not be true and induce others to spend energy debating what is factual.

For example, in a dialogue on Muslim-Christian relationships, it might be helpful to start by inviting several
speakers to give a factual overview of different teachings
and forms of both Christianity and Islam. This factual
overview can provide space for people with different experiences to recognize that they have only experienced
some forms of the other's religion, or have only heard
about some of the teachings.

In discussions on race relations, a central dynamic is
"How much has discrimination lessened since the bad
old days?" Findings from the
large-scale federally funded
studies of the prevalence of
housing discrimination might
be relevant. Similarly, longi-
tudinal studies that show the
softening of racialized atti-
tudes might also be relevant to such a discussion.

> **Facts can create
> an experience
> of surprise
> that bonds
> participants.**

In addition, little-known but relevant facts can create
a common experience of surprise for the participants
that can bond them.

Strategies for Presenting Facts

Facilitators can introduce facts near the beginning of
a dialogue process using a number of different strategies. Each has different implications for the process.
Some dialogues have combined more than one of the
following strategies.

a) Fact Sheet or Quizzes. A fact sheet with research
findings or an interactive quiz can be presented and re-
viewed fairly quickly. Fact sheets are particularly valuable for indisputable facts and when these facts might
play a role through the entire dialogue.

For example, in a Memphis, Tennessee, community dialogue about rising child obesity rates, facilitators distributed a fact sheet showing the prevalence of adolescent obesity, the general relationship between food and exercise, recent trends in the food industry, trends in schools, and factors of the physical environment. A quiz on surprising facts on the topic also gave participants a common experience.[11]

b] Audiovisuals. A short video can also play an important function. At the Memphis dialogue on obesity, facilitators used a short video featuring an adolescent reflecting on his struggle to lose weight. The video exposed the painful social dynamics of obesity and created an emotionally touching experience which bonded the participants. In large-scale dialogues with substantial budgets, organizers sometimes devote resources to producing audiovisuals to introduce topics.

c] In-Person Presentation. Authoritative leaders or experts can introduce facts through presentations. The Richmond dialogues on race began with a 40-minute PowerPoint presentation by a local scholar who had done extensive research on the ways that jurisdictional issues were contributing to racial and economic division in the city. In Fiji, the dialogue process included presentations by Christian, Hindu, and Muslim religious leaders emphasizing common religious teachings about peace.

Risks of Drawing Early Attention to "The Facts"

Presenting facts can distract from the dialogue process. Some members of the group will turn their attention to disputing your facts, especially if any of your facts are controversial. Some may begin to question whether the dialogue process is actually a neutral setting, or whether your depiction of relevant facts betrays the bias of the facilitator or organizers. If you choose to use facts, do so in a way that does not raise concerns even among skeptical participants.

If the factual presentation is experiential—such as watching a movie—the group may veer to talking about the experience of watching the movie rather than the issues that the movie highlights. This is another way that facts can distract a group from exploring its own experiences and perspectives. If this happens, the facilitator needs to refocus the group's attention on the dialogue's underlying issues.

The presentation should not cause any participant to feel attacked or defensive, as this generates unproductive resistance. This concern is particularly relevant in cases where the dialogue addresses issues of historical conflicts between groups. Typically, part of the dialogue's purpose is to move people past a tendency to think of other groups as the cause of ongoing tensions, and toward a shared responsibility.

> **Take care to present facts in a nonbiased way.**

Finally, some in the group may interpret an initial focus on facts as a signal that what matters in the dialogue is a proper analysis of the facts. Positioning facts early in the process makes it more difficult to reestablish participants' experiences as important sources of learning.

A Word About Key Concepts

Just as one must take care in presenting facts in a dialogue, it is also important to think through how to use key concepts. Defining concepts like "racism," "obesity," or "homosexuality" can be controversial. If your dialogue design or facilitation choices depend on a common definition of key concepts, the dialogue can be sidetracked by this discussion. Yet it can be dangerous for a facilitator to impose definitions of key terms on a group without discussion. A handout with a set of definitions from a range of scholars or public figures can be helpful to demonstrate a consensus or diversity of opinions. Facilitators can ask group members to agree on one definition.

Record-Keeping and Feedback

Dialogue makes it possible to gather insights from many people. It is important to find a way to unobtrusively gather the data from the group and distill the most important themes that help produce a sense of both the common ground and the diversity of opinion. Notes from different phases of the dialogue may be taken on large sheets of paper at the front of the room. The dialogue designers should decide ahead of time when it is appropriate to take public records of the dialogue, and when it would distract from group members listening to each other.

The task of collecting information is particularly challenging in large dialogues, as group reporting takes too long. AmericaSpeaks uses modern technology for this process, with each dialogue subgroup or table sending its information from a laptop computer to a central bank of computers for distillation. The primary themes from the dialogue are transmitted on a wireless network to a "theme team" that distills the main points of consensus among the participants. These themes are fed back to the entire group on large video screens, and each participant uses a keypad to vote on which of the themes or options for action are most important to him/her.

There are lower-tech ways as well. For example, subgroups can decide on a few top insights or conclusions from a conversation, and submit those to someone (maybe a lead facilitator) who discerns common points throughout the entire group.

Phase 4: Exploring Possibilities for Action

Ideally, dialogue processes prompt people to move from talk to action. The final phase of a dialogue explores the possibilities for action. Some groups may choose to express either personal or collective commitments to address the issues. If the dialogue has reached its potential for transformation, people often feel energized and motivated to enact change. Sometimes people begin projects or make plans to work together. Building relationships across lines of division and increasing understanding of a situation can help people see what needs to be done to address the issue and find ways to work together.

Depending on the dialogue's purpose and the group's internal dynamics, a focus on moving toward action could be a relatively short portion of the dialogue, an entire session, or a set of sessions. Regardless, it is important to help participants recognize that they have some degree of influence to change the situation and address the issue.

As the dialogue winds down, participants often value reflecting upon the process and sharing what they have learned. Even in the most contentious dialogues, most participants describe a positive effect. Facilitators may want to explicitly prompt positive responses by asking

"What are one or two positive things that you have gotten out of this process?"

Lastly, in this final phase, participants often want to express appreciation to each other. In many cases, this

---

Sample Questions for Action Planning

- What should we do about this issue now that we have built relationships with each other, shared our experiences, and deepened our understanding of the issues?

- What can we do individually and as a community to improve relationships among ourselves and address the needs in our community?

- Of all the ideas shared, which two or three ideas seem most practical for us to work on together?

- What resources do we already have available to us?

- If there are existing policy options on this issue, what do we think of these existing options? (Facilitators can offer a handout with three to five policy options to address the problem.)

- Which of these policies do you think will address everyone's needs in this issue?

- What other policy options can we brainstorm together?

---

happens naturally, with no prompting from the facilitator. But creating such an opportunity—without demanding more appreciation from people than they want to extend—is helpful in providing a sense of closure.

6.
Facilitating a Dialogue

The role of the facilitator may be the most important element of a dialogue. In fact, a skilled facilitator can often create an effective dialogue even if the other important elements are missing. Choosing a facilitator is critical.

"Natural leaders" or people who play important leadership roles in other activities may make excellent candidates for serving as facilitators, but not always. This chapter discusses competency skills for facilitators and explores how facilitators compare to other types of effective leaders.

Key Facilitation Skills and Tasks

Facilitation is a learned skill in which many people can become reasonably proficient. Following are some of the key tasks required of effective facilitators.

Establish the purpose of the dialogue.

Everyone in the room should clearly understand the purpose and focus of the dialogue. Put this in writing and say it verbally. Check that participants understand and ask if they have any questions.

Foster dialogue.

Remind participants of the difference between dialogue and debate. Help them grasp the importance of listening deeply and speaking respectfully and honestly, and how this differs from ways they may be used to talking with others.

Manage the agenda and guide the process.

Be as self-confident as possible to assure the participants that you know how to guide the process. Keep the discussion focused, and keep your focus on the process. Ask open-ended questions that explore the complexities of the issues.

Develop ground rules.

Either explain the ground rules or ask the group to develop them. Ask participants if they can agree to the rules, and invite them to monitor how well they are following them. When the ground rules are violated, give gentle but firm reminders.

Listen actively.

Demonstrate verbal and nonverbal listening skills that show people you understand what they are saying.

Monitor group dynamics.

Pay attention to ensure that everyone has a chance to speak and that no one is dominating the conversation. Check in with participants who seem quiet or withdrawn. Ask how they are feeling. Remind participants to "share air time" so that everyone feels responsible for monitoring the group's dynamics.

Communicate interest in everyone's perspective.

Help to bring out views that aren't represented. Participants in a dialogue should feel that the facilitator is authentically interested in understanding their experiences and ideas.

Help deal with difficult participants.

Keep one-on-one arguments from taking over. Prepare for participants who talk too much, refuse to participate, or disrupt the workshop. Respond to the situation with confidence and grace.

Summarize and paraphrase.

Help people feel that their unique experiences and ideas are heard and understood by summarizing and/or paraphrasing what is said. This skill can also help with long-winded participants who have lost their own key message.

Stay impartial.

In order to maintain everyone's trust, facilitators are very careful about sharing their experiences and usually refrain from expressing their beliefs relevant to the issue. The facilitator's role is to help participants wrestle with the similarities and differences in the views they express.

Model the behavior you expect from participants.

Facilitators should model deep listening, respectful and honest speaking, and other ground rules at all times through their words and body language.

Close with a summary.

Summarize the discussion and help focus the group on talking concretely about next steps they want to take individually and collectively.

Advanced Skills and Tasks

Some facilitator characteristics—whether learned or natural—are important in leading highly effective dialogues.

Facilitators inspire confidence in their leadership.

Dialogue requires a facilitator to lead the dialogue and decide where to guide the conversation next. For much if not most of the time, participants are so engrossed in the exchanges that they lose track of the larger flow of the dialogue process. On occasions where the group's attention is drawn to the process itself, it is important that the facilitator not appear incapable of making a decision. The group must feel that it can trust the facilitator's judgment, and that the facilitator trusts his or her own judgment.

Natural charisma to inspire confidence in others is useful in the facilitator's role as the leader on the journey. He or she will need to constantly make decisions about which topics and comments are important to pursue, and which are not. A personality that inspires trust certainly helps create an atmosphere that people feel is safe and productive.

Facilitators are good multi-taskers.

Facilitators need to keep track of many different and competing objectives at once. For example, articulate but long-winded speakers often bring important content to a discussion. But in order for a group to benefit from their contributions, a facilitator must keep track of the relative values of what they are saying, people's level of apparent boredom/interest in the ideas, how many people have yet to address the topic, and how much time is left in the session.

Facilitators are flexible and not overly controlling.

Since the facilitator's job is to create a setting in which many people feel empowered to listen, talk, and learn, the facilitator must be careful not to overly control the dialogue, because this will make people feel boxed in and not truly included. Facilitators provide guidance but also listen to the group and observe participants' level of energy when deciding whether to be flexible or keep on schedule.

Facilitators see a situation from many points of view.

Many facilitators engage in dialogue as part of their commitment to broader principles like justice, peace, and democracy. In some cases, competent facilitators have an unconscious (or even conscious) bias against participants that hold more political, economic, or social power. Facilitators need to do a great deal of self-reflection to process their own biases before facilitating a dialogue in which their biases might affect their ability to manage the process. Facilitators must be able to empathize with the experiences of all the participants. The capacity to understand all points of view is essential.

Facilitators stay calm and engaged.

One test of a facilitator's skill level is his or her reaction to emotional intensity within a group. This may take the form of anger, tears, rudeness, expressed frustration, or other intense emotion. In these conditions, a facilitator's primary task is to maintain the group's focus of attention in spite of the charged emotions. This can be very difficult, especially if the emotions are directed at the facilitator. Staying calm in the midst of anxiety or tension takes a great deal of practice and inner strength. A wise facilitator stays emotionally present and engaged while thinking about what is best for the group rather than formulating a defense or attempting to stop emotional expression.

Facilitators pose provocative questions.

A highly skilled facilitator uses the dialogue design as a guide and spontaneously asks questions of the group to move the dialogue forward and attain a deeper level of honest analysis. The ability to improvise and generate questions that help the group see commonalities or disagreements is an important skill. (See Chapter 5 for suggested questions facilitators might ask.)

Facilitators connect with people.

A final important quality of first-rate facilitators is the ability to emotionally connect with participants and continually invite them to stay engaged in the process. Highly skilled facilitators convey that they understand how participants see the issue, and that everyone in the group can learn more from each other by staying with the process. The challenge for facilitators is to stay engaged in the process as participants learn and transform at their own rate without seeming to be smarter or more evolved than the participants. The facilitator reminds participants that they all are on a path toward a higher understanding, and that the facilitator is only a half-step ahead.

Differences Between Facilitators and Other Leaders

Most natural leaders and facilitators share some important skills, but not all effective leaders make good facilitators. Some leadership roles and skills undermine the capacity to be good facilitators.

Teachers and trainers may be tempted to see their role as fostering growth and development by dispensing wisdom to the group. By contrast, effective facilitators recognize that the group must come to its own conclusions based on participants' exchanges.

Good meeting leaders stick to a defined agenda. However, effective facilitators must keep their focus on the overall goal of learning rather than accomplishing an agenda.

Good public speakers may be tempted to use their rhetorical skills to sway people to their points of view. But good facilitators help people understand all points of view, including their own.

7.
Moving from
Dialogue to Action

Dialogue is useful for information-gathering, analysis, relationship-building, and decision-making. Dialogue is also a method of social change.

While dialogue ideally leads to action, dialogue organizers and facilitators cannot mandate action. The goal of dialogue is to create greater understanding, which in turn may motivate participants to take action personally or collectively with others. It is important that participants "buy into" the idea of action themselves rather than feel morally coerced into it.

Though dialogue planners and facilitators cannot mandate action at the outset of a dialogue, they can create the space for it to happen. This chapter explores how to maximize the possibility that dialogue will successfully move toward real change.

The issue of standardized school tests provides a useful example of how dialogue might lead to actions that bring about social change. For immigrant students and their parents, standardized school tests designed for English-speaking youth may not accurately test intelligence or comprehension. If immigrant students and their families are isolated from other immigrant families, they may see this as an individual problem rather than a community problem (see Levels of Social Change). If a school decides to hold a dialogue on immigrant issues and school tests, people may recognize collective patterns and problems with the testing. Communities are nested within larger state and national structures and policies that affect educational funding and testing.

How and when does dialogue effectively translate into structural change? What is the "tipping point" for transforming an issue?[12] Does it require a critical mass that need to participate in a dialogue process in order to build relationships across the lines of a conflict and understand more deeply the issues involved? Or does it require the involvement of key community leaders in a dialogue process? What other tools are needed in addition to dialogue to bring about social change? An old saying states: "If the only tool you have is hammer, everything looks like a nail." The same holds true for

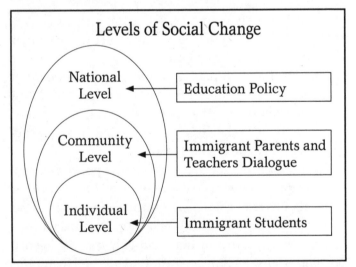

Levels of Social Change

National Level ← Education Policy

Community Level ← Immigrant Parents and Teachers Dialogue

Individual Level ← Immigrant Students

Developed by Marie Dugan and adapted with permission by John Paul Lederach in "From Issues to Systems" in the *Meditation and Facilitation Manual* (Mennonite Conciliation Services, 2000).

dialogue; it may not always be the most appropriate tool. Yet in most instances, dialogue is an ideal first tool.

Mahatma Gandhi and Martin Luther King both taught that dialogue should be tried first, before any other strategies. When Gandhi became determined to end British colonialism, he invited and engaged in dialogue with the British whenever he could. But he also understood that at many points along the journey, the British representatives were not interested in true dialogue but sometimes were just trying to dissuade him from pursuing change. Yet Gandhi kept to his principles. He pushed for change through a wide variety of nonviolent tactics and strategies, but took every opportunity to engage in dialogue with those who opposed him.

Balancing Power and Raising Awareness

Dialogue may not always be possible or productive if power is unbalanced and awareness of a conflict is low. Some people with political advantage may see dialogue as an opportunity to reach across the lines of conflict and bring people into their own political agenda. Often people within the more powerful group have little interest in meeting with members of the less powerful group. Those with less political advantage may see dialogue as passive, or even a distraction from the real work for change.

In Nashville, Tennessee, in the 1960s, African-American students couldn't get a meeting with the mayor to discuss racial integration. The students first had to balance the power between the white leaders and the black community. Black students increased their power by organizing, training themselves in nonviolent action, and carrying out sit-ins, marches, and boycotts of stores that promoted racial segregation. These actions brought media attention, public sympathy for their cause, and pressure on white leaders to do something about the boycotts, which were affecting white businesses. The nonviolent actions opened the door for successful dialogue between the black youth and the city leaders that led to desegregation.

The diagram below illustrates how methods like dialogue are better able to contribute to social change if power is roughly balanced between groups. Dialogue is more productive if participants from all sides of a con-

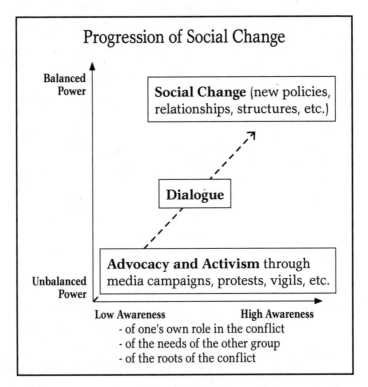

Progression of Social Change

Balanced Power

Social Change (new policies, relationships, structures, etc.)

Dialogue

Advocacy and Activism through media campaigns, protests, vigils, etc.

Unbalanced Power

Low Awareness   High Awareness
- of one's own role in the conflict
- of the needs of the other group
- of the roots of the conflict

Adapted with permission from Adam Curle, *Making Peace* (London: Tavistock Press, 1971).

flict are committed to better understanding the issues. As the diagram illustrates, when power is unbalanced and public awareness of an issue is low, it may be important to first raise public awareness and demonstrate collective power through petitions, marches, or some other type of symbolic action. Strategic and persistent advocacy—especially if it avoids framing the issue with a clearly defined set of villains—can increase the willingness of all groups to engage in dialogue.

More People *and* Key People

A project researching the effectiveness of dialogue, called the *Reflecting on Peace Project*, compared four different approaches for bringing about social change:[13]

The more-people approach aims to engage large numbers of people in processes to address an issue. Broad involvement of "the people" is seen as necessary to change.

The key-people approach involves certain important leaders or groups of people who are seen as opinion leaders and able to effect change in a situation.

The individual-level approach seeks to change the attitudes, values, perceptions, or circumstances of individuals as an important first step to bringing about real and lasting social change.

The structural-level approach more directly aims to change socio-political or institutional structures. These programs address the grievances that fuel conflict, and institutionalize nonviolent modes of handling conflict within society.

These researchers found that projects (including dialogue processes) focusing on change at the individual level without translating into action at the structural level have *little discernible effect* on addressing the broader political or social issues they seek to change.

In addition, the study found that approaches concentrating on including more people, but not necessarily key leaders or groups, did not constructively address social issues. Conversely, the research found that strategies focusing only on key people without including others were equally ineffective.[14]

If programs focus on one strategy only, they are unlikely to create social change. Programs that intentionally link individual with structural efforts, or include key people as well as more people are most likely to bring about change.

Designers of dialogue processes can assess how to include more people and key people, and intentionally plan for how individual change may impact the structural level.

From Dialogue to Action

Ideally, a dialogue process creates a space for people to build relationships and develop new networks that increase people's vision and desire to take collective action. Chapter 5 suggests types of questions that help people assess what they personally and collectively can do.

Creating enough time and space in the dialogue agenda for this phase is important. If people view the last action-planning phase of dialogue as an add-on or as something to get through after a long day, it is less likely to lead to effective action.

8.
Assessing Dialogue Effectiveness

People and organizations that utilize dialogue often do not spend energy or resources to evaluate its effectiveness. Increasingly this is changing as foundations and other entities require applicants to justify their requests for funding. Some regard dialogue as a soft activity that doesn't translate into institutional/structural change. For these reasons, it is important to conduct evaluations, even relatively simple ones, that demonstrate the impact of dialogue on people, groups, and structures.

Dimensions for Assessing Dialogue

What follows is a five-part framework to evaluate dialogues. In this framework, social interventions such as dialogue work by affecting participants on one or more of five dimensions: *knowledge, awareness, motivation, skills,* and *connections to others.*

Knowledge

What and how much new knowledge do participants gain through dialogue? This dimension concerns a participant's understanding of the central facts and concepts related to the issue. If dialogue designers use fact sheets, presentations, or audiovisuals to present facts, it may be possible to assess an increase in factual knowledge. These facts and concepts might include key distinctions, prevalence rates, or impacts of the issue on different groups. Factual knowledge can be measured through surveys about the causes and dynamics of the issues and topics discussed.

Awareness

This dimension concerns the way participants perceive the connection between their own behavior and the issue being discussed. Emotional intelligence is increasingly valued as much as—if not more than—factual knowledge. Increasing participants' awareness of their role in an issue, and their sense that they can affect change either individually or collectively, is a measurable impact of a dialogue. Changes in awareness can be measured by asking people to identify their own role in the issue before and after the dialogue.

Motivation

This dimension concerns the degree to which participants feel inclined to take action—whether by themselves or with others—to address a problem. Motivation can be measured by identifying the number of people who took individual or collective action as a result of the dialogue, and, if possible, the types and impacts of those actions.

Skills

Dialogue participants may learn or improve on a wide range of skills in the process. Their communication skills may improve as they practice respectful and careful listening, learn empathy, and speak diplomatically, honestly, and assertively. They may also increase their problem-solving skills. Participants may develop concrete ideas about what they might do to affect change in a situation. Skills can be measured by asking people to rate the growth of their personal communication and problem-solving skills.

Connection to Others

This dimension concerns the quantity and quality of relationships between people in the dialogue. In modern societies, meaningful connections tend to decrease, but the dialogue process ideally builds people's networks. Effective action to address a problem requires group cooperation. Connections to others can be measured by asking people if they have increased levels of email, phone, or personal contact after the dialogue, or are engaged in a group effort to foster change.

Data Collection Strategies

Data collection strategies fall broadly into two types: qualitative processes like *interviews* and quantitative tools like *surveys*.

Interviews

Interview-based strategies are often the most appropriate choice for assessing dialogue's impact. Yet measuring the impact poses many challenges. Evaluating internal shifts in participants' outlook, the ways people think and feel, is not reliably observed.

One challenge when using interviews is that dialogues often have a delayed effect on participants. Many people report that they didn't fully recognize how much their outlook had shifted until some time had passed. On the other hand, people's willingness to take time for an interview often declines quickly after the dialogue ends.

Surveys

The other major strategy for assessing dialogue's impact involves conducting a survey of participants. Some of the same dilemmas that apply to interviews apply to surveys. For example, the ideal time to access the greatest number of responses is at the end of the last session, even before people leave the room. On the other hand, responses that are completed 30, 60, or 90 days after a dialogue ends give a better indication of any long-term effects that the dialogue process had on participants. A further challenge with surveys taken during the last session is that it is impossible to assess whether the dialogue has affected people's actions or behaviors with respect to the problem.

Interview and survey strategies can be combined. One possibility is to use different data-gathering tools at different times. For instance, one could administer interviews or surveys at the conclusion of a dialogue, and also attempt to gather data about participants' experience at some interval after the experience ends.

It is important to accurately gauge people's willingness to participate in any assessment. Participants will perceive evaluations as primarily benefiting the facilitator or organizer, and they will give limited time and energy to any reflection process. Therefore, carefully consider how much data is necessary for your purposes. It doesn't make sense to bother participants with extensive evaluations if the data will go unused.

9.
Dialogue for a New Century

The world is becoming a smaller place. As people and societies in far-flung places grow more intertwined through immigration, trade, travel, and technology, what happens in one country, region, or population often impacts another. These growing realities of globalization present a new set of challenges for this century.

For example, efforts to combat global climate change must address energy consumption patterns in countries with widely different cultures, development levels, economies, and vulnerabilities to the problem itself. Decisions to drill for new oil in China affect the price of gasoline in Iowa. Killer diseases in one country can spread via airplanes to countless cities around the world. High unemployment, crime, and violence in one region can fuel terrorist movements that threaten people in another.

As the world shrinks through global interdependence, more people will experience cultural diversity in new ways, including interracial marriage and immigration. With this often comes an increased expectation to include minority voices in decision-making processes.

In this new century, a widespread capacity for dialogue is essential. Dialogue is especially suited to accommodate the challenges of including an increasing number of stakeholders in a decision-making process. It can increase understanding of other people's values, religious and cultural identities, life experiences, and perspectives. It can help both citizens and political leaders create the greatest number of "winners" and the fewest number of "losers" by developing a deeper understanding of the experiences and needs of diverse people. And it can harness the creative power of people working together to find the most amenable solutions for all stakeholders.

At the global level, dialogue will need to replace coercive diplomacy if political leaders want to address the root causes of conflicts in the Middle East and in other embattled regions. While some skilled international negotiators use elements of dialogue in their work, often state-sponsored or Track I diplomacy is based more on coercion and force rather than dialogue's characteristics of careful listening, understanding, and joint problem-solving.

International dialogue can often occur through religious, media, academic, or other civil-society leaders, often with great effectiveness. This is called Track II diplomacy. For example, in the spring of 2007, a delegation of U.S. church leaders met with Muslim leaders in Iran to dialogue on ways to prevent war between the two countries. This dialogue created a space for Christian leaders to apologize to Muslim leaders for the war in Iraq, the torture used in prisons like Abu Ghraib, and the number of civilian casualties. Researchers have verified that apologies like this have a significant influence on official negotiations, supporting a diplomatic outcome.[15]

Examples of Track II diplomacy are occurring in Kosovo, where journalists dialogue with each other about the impact of their reporting on that nation's ethnic conflict and the opportunities for peace. In Israel/Palestine, women's groups from both sides of the conflict dialogue about how they can build the foundation of peace together. In unofficial dialogue, religious leaders or journalists can exchange ideas, explore unconventional options for resolving conflicts, or simply gain greater understanding of the deeper issues involved in the conflict.

> **Dialogue is the essence of democracy.**

Track II diplomacy complements Track I or official diplomatic efforts and is more likely to include the elements and skills of dialogue. The dialogue of Track II diplomacy is often more able to get beyond the high-level politics and face-saving posturing characteristic of official diplomatic efforts.

Dialogue is about helping people think better *together*. It is the essence of democracy. The spirit of community care and civic action at the heart of healthy democracy requires that people participate in learning, understanding, and shaping decisions that affect their families, communities, regions, and nations.

We hope this book helps people in different contexts think about how they can communicate more effectively on difficult subjects. In the next century, our very lives may depend on how well we as individuals, communities, and members of humanity can creatively address the challenges before us with the tools of dialogue rather than with weaponry, coercion, or force.

Appendix:
Tools for Enlarging the Conversation

Two tools help groups move through challenging aspects of sustained dialogue processes. The Intent/Impact Tool helps analyze a past incident. The Environmental Scan helps parties collectively analyze an ongoing situation.

Intent/Impact Tool

This tool helps people who have different experiences of the same event. It is particularly useful for understanding a situation where one of the parties feels that the other has acted in a way that was offensive, rude, or otherwise inappropriate. A facilitator can follow these steps to use this tool:

1. If possible, tell a brief story that illustrates that there can be positive intent from one person, but a negative impact on the other person.

2. Describe these two patterns of response:
   a. If someone's actions have frustrated, hurt, or angered us, we tend to focus on the negative impact of the action on us, and often assume negative intent by the other person/group.
   b. If we receive feedback that our actions have frustrated, hurt, or angered someone, we tend to focus on the positive intent we had, and often

minimize the negative impact on the other person/group.

3. Ask participants to review a situation where there was a gap between intent and impact, and have them discuss their intentions as well as the impacts experienced at various points.

By helping each party see that they and the other party can both hold a piece of the truth, this tool helps people move people toward a larger picture of the situation they both are facing.

Environmental Scan

The Environmental Scan is a tool to help stakeholders analyze positive and negative aspects of the past, present, and future within a 2x2 matrix.[16]

	Past/Present	Future
Positive		
Negative		

The squares can be defined as follows: Past/Present and Positive are aspects of the situation that people want to maintain as Points of Pride. Past/Present and Negative are aspects of the situation that foster frustration or Complaints among stakeholders. Future and Positive represent Aspirations that people hope to create or enhance. Finally, Future and Negative represent the Feared New Problems that people hope never come into existence.

	Past/Present	Future
Positive	Points of Pride	Aspirations
Negative	Complaints	Feared New Problems

Stakeholders who want change (referred to here as "change advocates") focus their attention on Complaints and Aspirations. Conversely, stakeholders who do not want change (referred to here as "continuity advocates") focus their attention on Points of Pride and Feared New Problems. The conflict between change advocates and continuity advocates often poses an obstacle in dialogues, even though both sides may be making accurate, though incomplete, assessments of the system. The purpose of the tool is to help participants see the system in its full context, including their own perspectives on the system that they may overlook.

The essential steps to using this tool are as follows:

1. Frame the dialogue as an effort to examine all aspects of the system. Some stakeholders may benefit from a preliminary explanation of the 2x2 matrix. In other circumstances, it is sufficient to frame the conversation more simply. For example, the conversation can be framed as an attempt to "examine what we like, what we don't like, and how we want it to be in the future."

2. Solicit perceptions from all stakeholders by sequentially advancing through the matrix. The sequence should be Points of Pride, Complaints, Aspirations, and Feared New Problems. *It is most useful if all parties contribute at least 1-2 ideas to each quadrant.*

For groups of 10 to 60, have them sit in clusters of 5-8 people. People can go through the matrix one quadrant at a time, with each person adding ideas on an index card or post-it. Have each person write down 3-5 ideas, spending two minutes on each quadrant. The clusters can group their ideas by themes, and then each cluster can put its ideas on a large matrix. At the end of this process, the contributions of all the clusters will include a very broad view of how the people in the system view it.

Savvy use of the scan can help dialogue in three ways:

1. It can lessen the intensity of the conflict by giving participants a unified framework that helps them see their own truth in relation to others with different perspectives.

2. Often advocates of change as well as continuity can agree on the substance of the points made in each quadrant. The matrix helps stakeholders move toward a question they can work on together: How can we keep our Points of Pride, address Complaints, achieve our Aspirations, and avoid New Problems?

3. The themes from each quadrant often help the participants see issues that need more discussion. For instance, if one idea appears in Points of Pride as well as in Complaints, it will be clear to all stakeholders that they need to discuss further and define that idea.

Endnotes

1   See Deborah Tannen, *The Argument Culture: Moving from Debate to Dialogue* (New York: Random House, 1998).

2   Hope in the Cities, an international organization, began dialogues on race, economics, and jurisdiction issues in cities in North America and Europe in the early 1990s. See www.iofc.org/en/programmes/hic

3   Dialogue facilitated by Schirch, September 22-24, 2001 in Suva, Fiji.

4   Dialogue series facilitated by Campt from March to May, 2006 for the Alexandria, Virginia, public schools.

5   This dialogue skills capacity-building was part of a cultural competence training for the Inland Empire Health Program, in Riverside, California. The multi-session training took place between March and May, 2001.

6   The AmericaSpeaks 21st Century Town meeting places people in tables of 8-10 with each table having a trained facilitator and a laptop computer on a wireless network. The primary themes from the dialogue are transmitted on a wireless network to a "theme team" who distill the main points of consenses among the participants. These themes are fed back to the entire group on large video screens, and each individual person uses a keypad to vote on which of the themes or options for action are most important to them. See www.americaspeaks.org

7   This meeting took place on July 20, 2002; the primary sponsor was the Civic Alliance to Rebuild Downtown New York.

8   The Neighbor-to-Neighbor dialogue program lasted from November 2001 to March 2002. The program involved 45 meetings, 139 host organizations, and a total of 1,838 participants.

9   See Harold Saunders, *A Public Peace Process: Sustained Dialogue to Transform Racial and Ethnic Conflict* (New York: Palgrave, 1999).

10   For more detail on the symbolic role of space in dialogue processes, see Lisa Schirch, *Ritual and Symbol in Peacebuilding* (Connecticut: Kumarian Press, 2005).

11   The Memphis meeting on youth obesity was one of a series of regional meetings convened by Shaping America's Youth. This meeting included nearly 1,000 participants.

[12] See Malcolm Gladwell, *The Tipping Point: How Little Things Can Make a Big Difference* (New York: Little, Brown, and Company, 2002).

[13] See Mary B. Anderson et al., *Reflecting on Peace Practice Handbook* (Massachusetts: Collaborative for Development Action, 2004).

[14] Ibid.

[15] See Richard Bilder, "The Role of Apology in International Law and Diplomacy," *Virginia Journal of International Law* 46 (Spring 2006).

[16] The Environmental Scan was developed by Dr. Barry Johnson. His work is available at www.polaritymanagement.com.

Recommended Reading

Books

Abu-Nimer, Mohammed. *Dialogue, Conflict Resolution, and Change: Arab-Jewish Encounters in Israel* (New York: State University of New York, 1999).

Issacs, Walter. *Dialogue and the Art of Thinking Together: A Pioneering Approach to Communicating in Business and in Life* (New York: Random House, 1999).

Kegan, Robert and Lisa Laskow Lahey. *How We Talk Can Change the Way We Work: Seven Languages for Transformation* (San Fransisco: Jossey-Bass, 2001).

Saunders, Harold. *A Public Peace Process: Sustained Dialogue to Transform Racial and Ethnic Conflict* (New York: Palgrave,1999).

Yankelovich, Daniel. *The Magic of Dialogue: Transforming Conflict into Cooperation* (New York: Touchstone, 1999).

The following books in the *Little Books of Justice and Peacebuilding* series may be helpful as you plan and facilitate dialogues:

The Little Book of Circle Processes by Kay Pranis describes how to use Circle methodology for dialogue and decision-making. It contains helpful information about the process of setting guidelines and values. (Intercourse, PA: Good Books, 2005.)

The Little Book of Cool Tools for Hot Topics by Ron Kraybill and Evelyn Wright provides a toolkit of techniques that are useful for facilitating. (Intercourse, PA: Good Books, 2006.)

Web Resources

Several organizations in the United States publish dialogue guides on specific topics such as urban planning, education, and cultural and racial diversity. The websites of these organizations offer many additional free resources on how to organize and facilitate dialogue.

Public Conversations Project
www.publicconversations.org

The aim of the Public Conversations Project is to foster modes of communicating that lead to mutual understanding, respect, and trust. PCP convenes, designs, and facilitates dialogues, meetings, and conferences, and provides both customized and packaged training in related skills.

Study Circles Resource Center
www.studycircles.org

The Study Circles Resource Center is a national organization that helps local communities develop their own ability to organize large-scale and diverse dialogues to support and strengthen community change. Study Circles works with neighborhoods, cities and towns, regions, and states, paying particular attention to the racial and ethnic dimensions of the problems they address.

National Coalition on Dialogue and Deliberation
www.thataway.org

NCDD's mission is to bring together and support people and organizations in ways that expand the power of discussion to benefit society. NCDD provides resources, networking opportunities, and programs for those dedicated to solving group and societal problems through honest talk, quality thinking, and collaborative action. The NCDD website is a popular hub for practitioners and scholars in this emerging field, and houses an extensive collection of resources, news, events, and opportunities related to dialogue and deliberation.

AmericaSpeaks
www.americaspeaks.org

AmericaSpeaks develops innovative deliberative tools that give citizens an opportunity to have a strong voice in public decision-making. While the organization does consulting on citizen engagement and strategic planning, it is best known for its 21st Century Town Meetings, which allow hundreds or thousands of people—sometimes in physically disparate locations—to express their individual perspectives in a process that quickly and transparently summarizes the group's collective conclusions and priorities for action. While much of AmericaSpeaks' work has focused on connecting citizens to elected officials, the organization has also used this process for corporations, non-profits, and international organizations.

About the Authors

Lisa Schirch is a professor of peacebuilding at Eastern Mennonite University (EMU) in Harrisonburg, Virginia, and program director of the 3D Security Initiative (www.3Dsecurity.org), which promotes conflict prevention and peacebuilding in U.S. security policymaking. With colleagues in the Center for Justice and Peacebuilding at EMU, Schirch consults with a network of organizations involved in peacebuilding activities throughout the U.S., Latin America, Africa, Asia, and Europe. She has worked in over 20 countries.

A former Fulbright Fellow in East and West Africa, Schirch has written four books and numerous articles on conflict prevention and peacebuilding. She is a frequent public speaker and has TV and radio experience discussing U.S. foreign policy. She holds a B.A. in International Relations from the University of Waterloo, Canada, and a M.S. and Ph.D. in Conflict Analysis and Resolution from George Mason University.

David Campt is the founder of the The DWC Group (www.thedwcgroup.com), which is a group of experts who help corporations, non-profit organizations, communities, and universities harness the power of dialogue to make smarter decisions and become more inclusive. David has presented and enacted dialogue principles at board of director retreats as well as large meetings with 4,000 people in dynamic small-group conversations.

Often known as The RaceDoctor (www.racedoctor. org), David frequently provides his insights on race relations and institutional cultural competence to print and electronic media outlets as well as to members of Congress, Fortune 500 companies, museums, foundations, and international peacebuilding organizations. In the late 1990s, he served as Senior Policy Advisor at the White House for the President's Initiative on Race. David holds an undergraduate degree from Princeton University, and Master's and Doctorate degrees from the University of California at Berkeley.

Contacting the Authors

The authors would love to hear from you. If you want to offer feedback on this book or share how you have used dialogue, please send an email to bookofdialogue@yahoo.com.

METHOD OF PAYMENT

Check or Money Order
(payable to *Skyhorse Publishing* in U.S. funds)

Please charge my:

    MasterCard   Visa
    Discover   American Express

\# _____

exp. date _____
Signature _____

Name _____
Address _____
City _____
State _____
Zip _____
Phone _____
Email _____

SHIP TO: (if different)
Name _____
Address _____
City _____
State _____
Zip _____

Call: (212) 643-6816
Fax: (212) 643-6819
Email; bookorders@skyhorsepublishing.com
(do not email credit card info)

Group Discounts for

The Little Book of Dialogue for Difficult Subjects
ORDER FORM

If you would like to order multiple copies of *The Little Book of Dialogue for Difficult Subjects* by Lisa Schirch and David Campt for groups you know or are a part of, please email bookorders@skyhorsepublishing.com or fax order to (212) 643-6819. (Discounts apply only for more than one copy.)

Photocopy this page and the previous as often as you'd like.

Quantity   Price   Total

_____ copies of *Dialogue for Difficult Subjects* @ _____ _____

The following discounts apply:

1 copy	$5.99
2-5 copies	$5.39 each (a 10% discount)
6-10 copies	$5.09 each (a 15% discount)
11-20 copies	$4.79 each (a 20% discount)
21-99 copies	$4.19 each (a 30% discount)
100 or more	$3.59 each (a 40% discount)

Prices subject to change.

(Standard ground shipping costs will be added for orders of less than 100 copies.)